SMELL

A TRUE BOOK®

by

Patricia J. Murphy

Children's Press®

A Division of Scholastic Inc.

New York Toronto London Auckland Sydney
Mexico City New Delhi Hong Kong
Danbury, Connecticut

A young girl uses her nose to smell perfume.

Reading Consultant
Nanci R. Vargus, Ed.D.
Assistant Professor
Literacy Education
University of Indianapolis
Indianapolis, IN

Content Consultant
Beth Cox
Science Learning Specialist
Horry County Schools
Conway, SC

Dedication:
To A.M.A

Library of Congress Cataloging-in-Publication Data

Murphy, Patricia J., 1963–
     Smell / by Patricia J. Murphy
     p. cm. — (A true book)
Includes bibliographical references and index.
Summary: Explores the sense of smell made possible by the nose as well
as its relationship to the sense of taste.
ISBN 0-516-22598-7 (lib. bdg.)   0-516-26969-0 (pbk.)
     1. Smell—Juvenile literature. 2. Nose—Juvenile literature. [1. Smell.
2. Nose. 3. Senses and sensation.] I. Title. II. Series.
QP458 .M87 2003
612.8′6—dc21   2001008340

1 2 3 4 5 6 7 8 9 10 R 12 11 10 09 08 07 06 05 04 03

Contents

You are surrounded by smells every morning, noon, and night.

Everyone Smells

When you wake up in the morning, you breathe in the new day. With every breath, you smell your clean shirt. You smell the cinnamon in your oatmeal too. You smell your mother's perfume— and it is only 8 A.M.! Your nose was busy before you even opened your eyes. The nose's work is never done. It is busy with every breath you take.

Your nose has two important jobs. Its first job is to help you breathe. Your nose forces air through its long narrow tubes, or nostrils, to your lungs. It warms and filters the air you breathe.

Your nose's second job is to smell. When you smell a flower, your nose picks up smell molecules in the air. Almost everything has smell molecules. They break off from things around you.

With every breath you take, air and smell molecules pass through

The small blue, red, and green clusters are an illustration of smell molecules traveling from the rose to the girl.

your nostrils. This mixture is forced up to your nasal cavity where your smell organs are. Most of the air and smell molecules travel on to the back of your mouth and throat. They finally go to the lungs.

The rest of the smell molecules travel to the **olfactory organs**. These organs are two small patches behind the bridge or top of your nose. They are the size of your thumbnail. Together, they do all your nose's smelly work.

Your olfactory organs send **nerve impulses**, or messages, to the brain's olfactory center in the **cerebral cortex**. This part of your brain can identify more than ten thousand smells. When the nerve impulses reach this area, the brain says, "What a beautiful flower!"

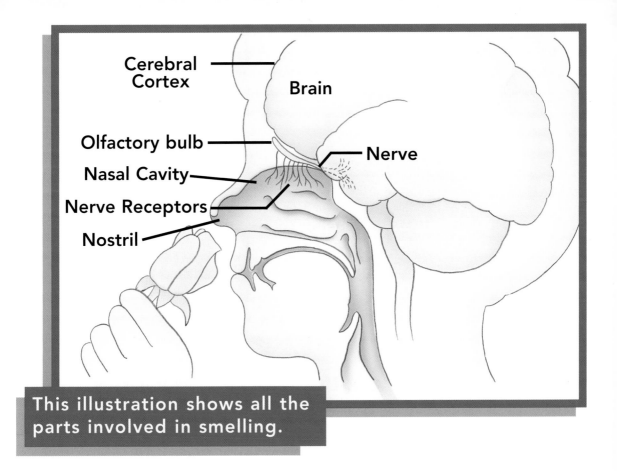

Cerebral Cortex

Brain

Olfactory bulb

Nerve

Nasal Cavity

Nerve Receptors

Nostril

This illustration shows all the parts involved in smelling.

Of all your five senses, smell is the simplest and fastest. Also, your sense of smell has the straightest path. A smell from the outside world goes straight to your brain.

The Nose Knows

Your nose is in the middle of your face. It is made of bone and **cartilage**. Your nose may be short or long. The tip of your nose may be round or pointed. It may have freckles or moles. The outside of your nose may look different than your friends' noses. On the

While people's noses may look different on the outside, inside their noses are the same.

inside, however, noses are all the same.

Your nose's olfactory organs are covered with millions of **nerve receptors**. These nerve receptors are cells that catch the smell molecules in their liquid or **mucus**. The receptors' tiny sensory hairs reach out and touch the smell molecules. The nerve receptors recognize the smell molecules.

Next, the nerve receptors change the smell molecules

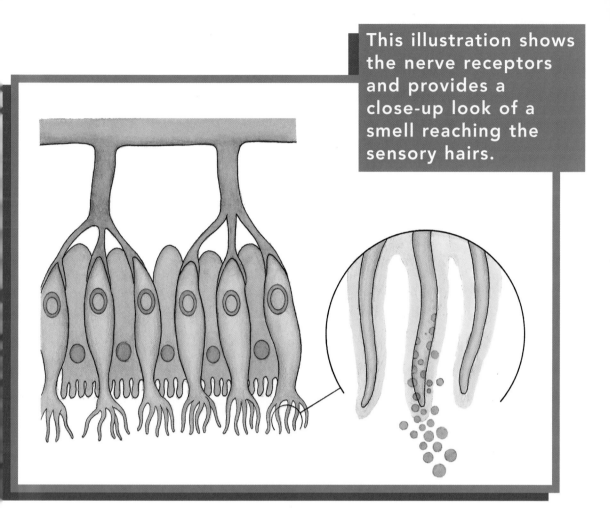

This illustration shows the nerve receptors and provides a close-up look of a smell reaching the sensory hairs.

into nerve impulses. These impulses travel along the nerve receptors' **nerve fibers**. They go up through the

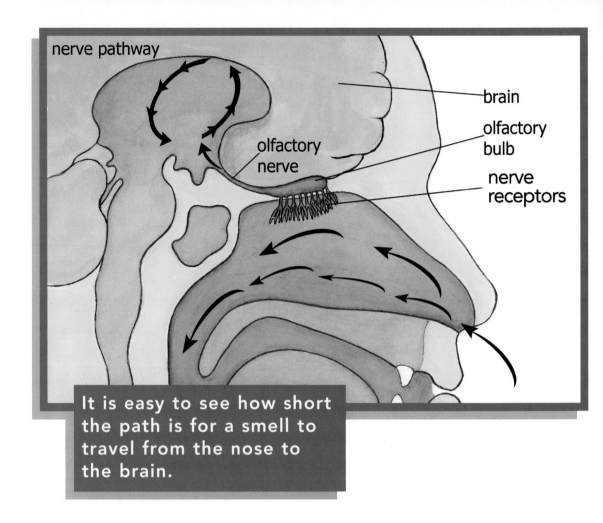

nerve pathway

brain

olfactory
bulb

olfactory
nerve

nerve
receptors

It is easy to see how short
the path is for a smell to
travel from the nose to
the brain.

bones of your skull to the
brain's **olfactory bulbs**. The
olfactory bulbs are groups of
nerve fibers in the brain.

Nerve impulses travel along these nerve fibers. On the way, they stop at the olfactory bulbs' message centers. These message centers sort out all of the impulses. Next, the nerve impulses travel to the olfactory center of the cerebral cortex. There, the brain identifies the nerve impulses as smells.

Scientists are not sure how nerve receptors recognize smell molecules. They are

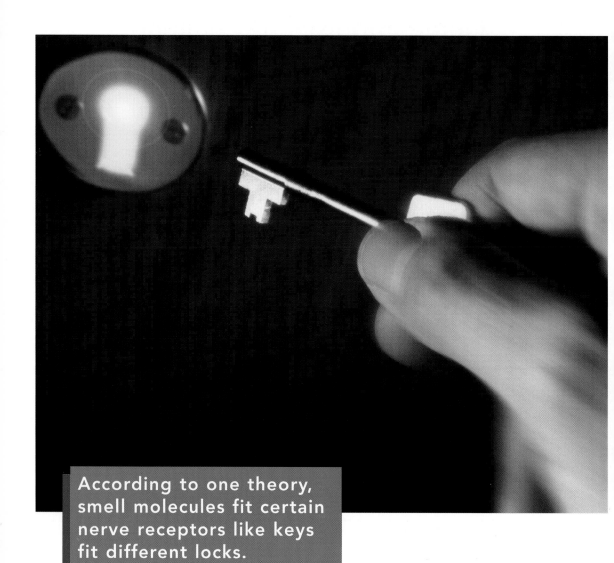

According to one theory, smell molecules fit certain nerve receptors like keys fit different locks.

working to learn more about smell. Some scientists have an idea or theory. It is called the Lock and Key theory. This theory says that every smell molecule fits a certain nerve receptor. The molecules act like keys. The receptors act like locks. Together, a lock and key set off a nerve impulse. This impulse is sent to the brain where it is recorded in your memory.

Remember Me?

For many people, certain smells trigger memories For example, when Stella smells fresh baked bread she thinks of her grandmother. She remembers the times that her grandmother baked bread. When Matthew smells sweaty socks, he thinks of gym class.

Scientists say these smell-related memories do not happen by chance. They believe our nerve impulses travel through areas of the brain that affect memory and feeling. Scientists are still studying the smell and memory connection.

Smell and Taste

When you bite into a hot dog, you taste the meat, the ketchup, the mustard, and the relish. So your taste buds are very busy. Your nose is busy too. These senses work closely together. Scientists say that 75 percent of taste is really smell.

The senses of taste and smell work together when you eat.

When you're sick, your sense of taste is affected by your stuffy nose.

Try this yourself. Hold your nose and bite into a cookie or taste an orange when you have a cold. Without your nose, foods like potatoes and apples taste the same.

Yuck! Eating isn't as tasty or as fun.

Your sense of smell helps make your food taste good. It also helps your appetite. When you smell food, you get hungry. Once your body

The smell of food often encourages you to eat.

smells food, your mouth makes a liquid called saliva. Saliva breaks down food so that your body can digest it, or pass it down to your stomach and intestines.

With each bite, your food mixes with saliva. Some of the food particles float up to your nasal cavity and olfactory organs. As you eat, you also smell, but the brain gets only one message. When taste and smell work together, you taste the flavors of food. Without

Even before you take a bite, your sense of smell tells your body to get ready for food.

smell, you would taste only four or five tastes. These tastes are sweet, sour, salty, and bitter. Some people say you would taste meaty too. When smell and taste work as a team, you can enjoy anything you have a taste—and smell—for!

Smell This! Scent Developers at Work

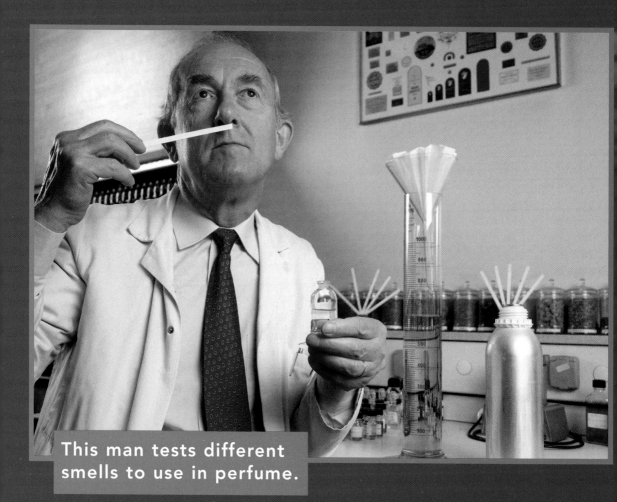

This man tests different smells to use in perfume.

Scent developers work with their noses. Some mix scents for perfumes, soaps, and bath products. Others create scents for household cleaners. They test these scents with special papers or blotters as well as on human skin.

To keep her olfactory organs in shape, Karen Khoury, a scent developer for Estée Lauder, washes with scent-free soap. She never eats garlic. She also takes walks to clear her nose. She trained her nose by sniffing the world around her!

When a Nose Can't Smell

Many things can spoil your sense of smell, such as colds, allergies, and injuries. For example, when you have a cold, your nose often becomes plugged up. Then you cannot breathe through your nose or smell.

Colds and allergies affect the olfactory organs. These health

Having a cold can limit your ability to smell.

problems can cause the nasal cavity to swell and fill up with mucus. Then smell molecules cannot get through to your olfactory organs and you cannot smell or taste anything.

Don't worry! When you get better, your sense of smell will return.

People who suffer injuries to nerve receptors are unable to smell. Smell molecules can still travel to the injured nerve receptors. The nerve receptors, however, cannot send smell nerve impulses to the brain. Many of these people will smell again. The nose makes new nerve receptors every four to five weeks.

Taking certain medications can cause problems with your sense of smell.

People who take certain prescription drugs, smoke cigarettes, or take cancer treatments also have trouble smelling things. When people grow older, their sense of smell grows weak. Some people are unable to smell certain odors or to detect musk in perfume, for example. Scientists are still trying to find out just why this happens.

Some accidents and injuries can hurt a person's sense of smell forever. These accidents and injuries hurt nerve fibers that carry the smell nerve impulses to the brain. Then the brain cannot receive these nerve impulses.

Having little or no smell affects taste. People who lose their sense of smell, also lose their sense of taste. They lose their nose for danger too. Without the sense of smell, people cannot smell smoke. They cannot tell if food has gone bad either. These people need to put more smoke alarms in their homes. They must always read the dates on food packages too. They must use their other senses to keep safe and healthy.

Your sense of smell can let you know when food has gone bad.

Sometimes, all noses stop smelling things. This is called smell fatigue. The nerve receptors in the nose can get their fill of some smells. Once you smell a freshly baked cookie, you stop smelling it. You can smell other smells but not the cookie! Your nose just needs a break before you can smell the cookie again.

Take Care of Your Nose

You have two eyes and two ears, but only one nose. It is important to take care of that nose. If you don't, your nose could stop sending sweet smells to your brain.

To keep your nose in tip-top shape, you need to take a few

Be kind to your nose when blowing it.

steps. Your sense of smell depends on it!

• Blow your nose gently. Always blow one nostril at a time. If you do not, you could hurt your nose's nerve receptors.

• Do not put things in your nose. These things can get stuck in your nasal cavity or olfactory organs. They could block your smelling and breathing.

• Lift, pinch, and cover a bloody nose. Keep very still. Taking these steps will help stop a nosebleed.

• Keep your nose away from harmful or strong chemicals, such as ammonia. Open windows when you paint or when you clean your home.

• Do not smell anything unknown. Do what scientists do! "Waft" or fan your hand over the top of a "smell." This will give you a tiny smell of it!

• Do not smoke. Smoking is bad for your lungs and it can also hurt your sense of smell. Smoking dulls your nose's nerve receptors. Smokers cannot smell as well as non-smokers can.

Wearing helmet protects your head from harm.

• Wear a helmet when you ride your bike or play sports. A helmet can prevent head injuries.

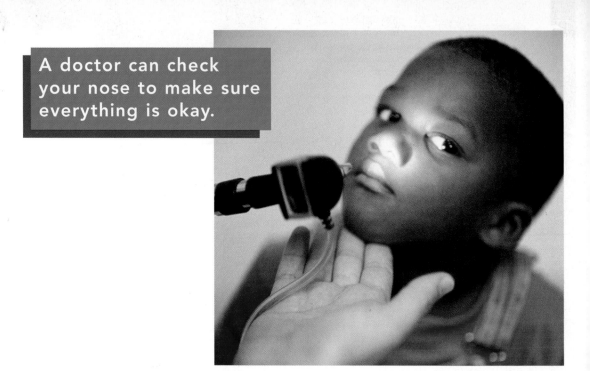

• Go to a doctor if you have a bad cold. Sometimes, nerve receptors in the nose can become infected.

• Stop and smell the roses. In other words, don't miss the wonderful smells all around you.

Facts About Smell

- Our sense of smell is 10,000 times greater than our sense of taste.

- The nose has millions of nerve receptors, but only one thousand different kinds! Each may fit only certain shaped smell molecules!

- The force of a sneeze has been clocked at 100 miles (161 kilometers) per hour.

- We sometimes sneeze to protect our nose and lungs from strong or harmful smell molecules.

- The sense of smell is the strongest when people are babies!

- It grows weaker when people get older.

- Bloodhounds can smell 1,000 times better than humans can.

- Insects have the greatest sense of smell.

- Some insects smell through holes in their antenna.

To Find Out More

Here are additional resources to help you learn more about the sense of smell.

 **Books**

Ballard, Carol. **How We Taste and Smell.** Raintree Steck-Vaughn, 1998.

Hartley, Karen, Chris Marco, and Philip Taylor. **Senses: Smelling Things.** Heinemann Library, 2000.

Hurwitz, Sue. **The Library of the Five Senses and the Sixth Sense: Smell.** Rosen Publishing, 1997.

Parker, Steve. **Young Science Concepts and Projects: The Body.** Gareth Stevens Publishing, 1998.

Pluckrose, Henry. **Exploring Our Senses: Smelling.** Gareth Stevens Publishing, 1995.

Pringle, Laurence. **Explore Your Senses: Smell.** Marshall Cavendish, 2000.

Organizations and Online Sites

How the Body Works
http://www.kidshealth.org

Learn all sorts of healthy things about your nose and the rest of your body.

Seeing, Hearing, and Smelling the World
http://www.hhmi.org/senses/

This online site has lots of information on the brain and the senses.

Neuroscience for Kids
http://faculty.washington. edu/chudler/chsense.html

Learn about all of five senses. Do fun things with your senses!

Human Anatomy Online
http://www.innerbody.com/ htm/body.html

Learn about the human body. See 100 different images.

Your Gross and Cool Body: The Sense of Smell
http://www.yucky.kids. discovery.com/noflash/body/ pg000150.html

Get answers to your questions about your nose and more!

45

Important Words

cartilage the soft tissue of the nose

cerebral cortex the outside layer of neurons or nerve cells on the brain, it allows us to see, think, feel, plan, and move

mucus a liquid or fluid that protects the inside of your nose

nerve fiber a thin fiber that sends messages between the brain and the spinal cord to let you see, feel, smell, and move

nerve impulse an electrical reaction sent along a nerve to the brain

nerve receptor a cell that sends information to other nerve cells, muscles, or glands

olfactory bulb the brain's smell relay station, it sends information to the olfactory center of the cerebral cortex

olfactory organ one of two patches of smell nerve receptors that recognizes smells

Index

Meet the Author

Patricia J. Murphy writes children's storybooks, nonfiction books, early readers, and poetry. She also writes for magazines, corporations, educational publishing companies, and museums. She lives in Northbrook, IL. She loves the scent of flowers, spring rains, and babies.